C000180161

KEEPING HOPE

FAVOURITE PRAYERS
FOR MODERN LIVING

Michel Quoist

Gill & Macmillan

Gill & Macmillan
Hume Avenue
Park West
Dublin 12
www.gillmacmillanbooks.ie

Originally published in French as
Garder Confiance; Les Plus belles Prières de Michel Quoist.
© Les Editions d'Atelier, Paris, 2013
© Translation, Gill & Macmillan, 2014

978 07171 6353 3

Design and print origination by OK Graphic Design, Dublin
Printed and bound by CPI Group (UK) Ltd, CR0 4YY

This book is typeset in Sabon 11/15 pt.

*The paper used in this book comes from the wood pulp of managed
forests. For every tree felled, at least one tree is planted, thereby renewing
natural resources.*

All rights reserved.
No part of this publication may be copied, reproduced or transmitted in
any form or by any means, without written permission of the publishers.

CONTENTS

SECTION 3: TO HOPE IS TO BE OPEN

SECTION 1

FINDING HOPE

Accepting yourself as you are

Perhaps you are in poor health, or you have little education, or you have a disability, or you are unattractive, or you lack a winning personality. Or perhaps your family has never encouraged you or helped you to satisfy your personal needs and desires. Perhaps your friends don't understand you, or perhaps you feel that you are getting nowhere at work when you could be making something of yourself. In short, your possibilities are limited by your own defects and an unsympathetic environment, so naturally you are discouraged and ready to give up. Take a good look at yourself: you have never really accepted your limitations. The proof? The thought often occurs to you: *If I were in good health, I'd...; If others understood me, I'd be able to...; If...* Your whole life is prefaced by ifs. Yours is a life dominated by envy of others and by personal despair. Do you often find yourself saying: *Sure, he can do it but not me...; If I had his brains, his education and his personality...; If...* Is there a spiteful tone and a note of rancour in your voice directed at yourself, your environment and life in general?

As long as you refuse to accept yourself as you are, you will never be able to build a full life for yourself because you will spend all your time wishing you had the tools that others have to build their lives without recognising what you already have at your disposal. Your tools may be different, but they can be just as good for your purposes. Don't worry about having the tools others have – find out what your own are and get down to work. Don't refuse to acknowledge your limitations; that would be disastrous. To deny their existence doesn't make them go away. If they do exist, ignoring them would give them the opportunity to undermine and destroy your life. Instead, accept them as they are, neither exaggerating nor minimising them.

If there is something you can change, what are you waiting for? Get busy, but with a calm perseverance. If there is something you can't change, accept it as it is. It's not a matter of resigning yourself to your fate by hanging your head in despair. You have to learn to lift it up and say yes to reality. Don't let yourself be bested by it. Bear it and offer it to God. Rest assured that God sees you and that in his eyes you are no more and no less the object of his love than those whom you presently envy. Place your cares, your sufferings, your sorrows in his hands. Believe more confidently in his strength and less in your own ability to cope with your problems. Recognise your limitations, accept them and offer them to him. You will discover that your poverty has become the very source of your wealth.

Your limitations are not simply obstacles to your success – they are also indications from God of the path your life is to take. Maybe you are not much of a conversationalist. Is this perhaps a sign that you should learn to be a good listener? Perhaps you are shy. Rather than trying to impose yourself on others and dominate them, you should make your life one of genial hospitality and graciousness. If you are not as smart as you'd like to be, this may mean that your life is meant to be one of more intense activity, etc. Recognise, accept and offer your limitations, but do the same with your possibilities for development as well.

You have some strong points too, and it is not a sign of humility to think that you are completely devoid of any; rather, it's either sheer pretence or mere nonsense. To acknowledge the gifts that the Lord has bestowed upon us is not a bad thing. Pride enters into the picture when we are under the impression that we have merited or acquired these gifts by ourselves. The genuinely humble man fears nothing, not even himself. He is not afraid of acknowledging his accomplishments or his limitations. He is not afraid of others, nor is he afraid of his environment. His only fear is the fear of the Lord, which is the beginning of wisdom.

When you receive a gift from a friend, you usually open the package immediately, admire your gift, indicate your approval and thank the giver. Your heavenly Father has given you many different gifts, but all too often you do not even dare to look at them and enjoy them. You play the saint and you don't even take the trouble to be polite to the Giver. The gifts of your heavenly Father aren't solely for your own personal use. They were given to you for others and for him as well. If you have received more, more will be expected of you. If you have anything to fear, it's not the acknowledgement of your gifts, but your failure to use them.

Accept yourself, but accept yourself in relation to others. Why are you afraid of your boss or your fellow workers, of anyone who is more intelligent than you, of anyone who can express themselves better than you, who knows more about the subject than you? Why do they make a favourable impression on you? Why are you so shy? Why are you paralysed by your feelings of inferiority? Precisely because you have not accepted yourself as you are in relation to others and because you are afraid of what others will think. If you are afraid of others, remember that you will only begin to make a good impression on them if you accept yourself as you are, for you can never be the other. In developing your own personality, you complement the personalities of others.

Don't try to live somebody else's life; it's just not you. The Father has given each of us a life to live. Trying to live somebody else's life is like trying to wear somebody else's clothes because they look good on them. Don't worry about what others think. They will accept your limitations if you are willing to acknowledge them. They will reject you, however, if they sense that you are ashamed or afraid and that as a result you are trying to deceive them by pretending to be something that you are not. Don't be afraid to say I don't know, I'm not able to do that, I don't understand. In this way you will be doing a service for others – they need someone who has the courage to acknowledge their limitations, for they will then find the courage to recognise and acknowledge their own.

Be yourself. Others need you just as the Lord has willed you to be. You have no right to put on a false face, to pretend you are what you're not, unless you want to rob others. Say to yourself: I am going to bring something new into this person's life because they have never met anyone like me, nor will they ever meet anyone like me, for in the mind of God I am unique and irreplaceable.

All of us are incomplete in some way. It is the union of all men and women who constitute the human family and it is their union in Christ that constitutes the Mystical Body. Your limitations are an invitation to union with all other men and women, a union rooted in love. Have but one desire: to be fully, without reservation, what God wants you to be, and then you will be perfect.

The Christian Response

It would be so easy...

M*any activists in the Church today are tired. They find themselves up against so many difficulties and misunderstandings that they want to draw back and take a rest.*

Then again, there are young people who announce that they have no intention of doing as their parents did. They want to have time to live, time for themselves.

Finally, some of the most committed people think that they may even be on the wrong road, that they ought to pray more and leave the action to God.

This is a serious state of affairs. God did not give us a world 'off the shelf'; he gave it to be created by us. Christians cannot retire to their tents and refuse to take on this task. More than any others, they are called to take it on, according to their abilities. This is truly authentic love for their brothers and sisters.

To have a living faith does not mean that we run away from the building site to ask God to do our work for us. It means that we give all our energies to the job at hand while asking God to work with us.

It would be so easy, Lord,
to abandon the struggle for a better world...
    this world which is still being born!
It would be so easy

to give up the exhausting meetings,
   the discussions,
   the reports,
the innumerable actions and commitments
   that are supposed to be essential
and the evenings of utter weariness,
   when I am more and more doubtful
   about how they can possibly help my brothers and
   sisters.

   It would be so easy
to listen to those voices around me,
voices that seem wise, friendly
   and even affectionate,
voices saying to me:
   'You're getting excited',
   'You're banging your head against a wall',
   'You're missing the point';
   voices whispering insidiously behind my back:
   'He enjoys that',
   'That's his temperament',
   'He doesn't like to be passed over.'

   It would be so easy
to give way to discouragement
and to dress it up in the good and pious intentions
   of forgotten obligations
   and broken promises.

It would be so easy then
to withdraw to my own home,
to have free evenings again,
and weekends to enjoy,
    and children's laughter,
    and my wife's arms.

It would be so easy to sit down
and bandage my wounds after too many hard fights,
    to rest my tired legs,
    my arms, my head
    and my heart,
and to find peace far from the din of battle,
and to listen at last to the silence
    in which you speak to the faithful – so they say –
    far away from the noise.

It would be easier, Lord,
to stand aside and not get my hands dirty,
to watch others fighting and debating,
to advise them and to complain about them,
to judge them and to pray for them.
    It would be easier…
    but I ask you, Lord,
is that really what you want of me?
    I no longer know.
    I no longer know.

Lord, enlighten me, help me.
I no longer know what I should do,
because in the concert of voices around me,
    wise voices,
    friends' voices,
    and those of my dear ones,
I often hear another voice,
    deeper and more serious,
    challenging me, persistently,
    in the depths of my troubled heart:
'You are taking the Lord's place.
Only he can change men and women and the world.
    Abandon yourself to him
    and he will do what you,
    in your arrogance,
    thought you were capable of doing.'

Is this your voice, Lord?
    I don't know any longer.
    I don't know any longer.
    But if this is really what you want, this evening,
    I place my resignation in your hands!

I refuse to accept your resignation, says the Lord,
    Don't listen to your voices,
    they don't come from me.
    I will never take your place,
    because it is I who have given it to you.

Nothing will be done without you and without your
    brothers and sisters,
because I have wanted you to be responsible together
    for humankind and for the world.
But nothing will be done without me either...
and perhaps you have forgotten that.

Go now, little one, and sleep in peace,
    and tomorrow,
    you and I,
    I and you,
    together,
    both of us with your sisters and brothers,
    we will take up the struggle again.

Pathways of Prayer

Prayer from the depths of my solitude

God is a 'subsisting relationship'; Father, Son and Holy Spirit are so united that they are one. Human beings, male and female, created in the image of God, also exist in relationships, but they are not complete and perfect. They must create themselves gradually in relationships of understanding, respect and love with all other human beings and particularly with those close to them. However, one of the great dramas in today's world is the breakdown of human relationships. People are crowded into towns, apartment buildings and public transport and often live side by side without ever really knowing each other. This is why so many people are lonely, especially the elderly, the sick, the handicapped and prisoners. This is very serious, because if men and women have no relationships with others, they slowly destroy themselves and can die from loneliness. People waiting for somebody to join them in the depths of their solitude may have to wait for a long time. The only way they can overcome their solitude is by coming out of themselves and going towards others. Jesus Christ is with them, Jesus who came so that all humanity might be made into one body in him.

I'm alone,
alone, Lord, do you understand?
   Alone
   and there's a party going on outside.

I turned off the radio,
which so often creates the illusion of a presence,
    but suddenly
    silence filled the room
and anguish sneaked into my heart
   and stayed there.

For a moment I listened
   to some noises on the stairs.
I imagined that I heard footsteps...
somebody coming up?
   What's the point of this foolish hope,
   since I'm not expecting anyone
   ...and nobody will come!

Lord, if you wanted to,
you would send me somebody!
   I need somebody,
I need a hand, Lord,
   only a hand on my hand,
   resting there like a bird;
I need lips on my forehead
   and the warmth of a kiss;

a glance,
    just a glance
    to prove to me
that at least I exist for someone;
a few words,
    and in these words
    a person caring for me.

    But nobody will come.
    I'm alone.
    Alone.
    And there's a party going on outside.

Yes, you can speak, Lord,
and I'm really listening!
But I've heard it all before
    and the priests have told me the same thing:
'You are not alone' because 'I am there'.
Yes, you are there,
    but without lips,
    without a glance towards me and without words.
And I'm not an angel,
    since you gave me a body!

Have you nothing else to say, Lord?
    Do you not speak either?
    Are you angry?

I have been a prisoner in my loneliness for a long time,
    and crossword puzzles
    or their squares
    can't be turned into a door
    through which I can escape
from my undeserved imprisonment.

But all of a sudden I think,
or perhaps it is you speaking to me again,
    I think that I'm not the only one
    languishing in solitude.
    I know some of them live near me,
    and I know this harsh world
where there are millions of people,
bodies crowded together
in apartment buildings or in the crowd,
    living beside each other,
    rubbing shoulders,
    knocking against each other,
    without ever meeting each other.
This is not what you wanted, Lord,
you who said that you came
to gather your scattered children
    and to make them into one family.

Now, Lord, my suffering
tells me a lot about the suffering of others,
and I hear their cries,

which are louder than my own,
and I understand at last
    that there is only one remedy
    that can heal my solitude:
    it is to reach out to others
    and heal their loneliness.

I've found my vocation, Lord!
I, who so often felt useless
    and capable of so little
    despite my anxiety to be helpful:
I'll be a maker and mender in the Church.

I'll try to tighten links that were loose
    and perhaps renew
    some that were broken.
I'll repair a little of the fabric of the family,
and since on this earth, Lord, you no longer have
    hands, lips,
    glances and words,
I offer myself as substitute
    for all those whose need, like mine,
    is for a body,
    even an ageing body,
to tell them that they are not alone
and that Somebody loves them.

Goodbye, loneliness!
It's late this evening, Lord, but I promise you
    that tomorrow
I'll begin my work
by going to visit my neighbour.
    Good night, Lord…
    bereft of kisses,
    once again
    I have nothing to return,
but tomorrow I'll be ready with a kiss
and I'll be able to give it.

Pathways of Prayer

I need to know that I am useful

He said: 'I need to know that I am useful.' I understand him only too well. Who could live without a reason for living? Useless things are usually thrown away.

The best thing I can do for others is to help them discover a purpose to their lives.

I'll never stop believing in people. I'll never stop believing that each one of us is indispensable and irreplaceable, because we are all unique. I'll never be attentive enough to others, open to them, silently imploring: I need you. Enrich me, because until you came along I was poor.

With Open Heart

I'm growing old, Lord

Old age can be a trial. Even though life is often difficult, many of us try to hold onto it when it begins to slip away. The worst suffering is to feel that you are useless and that you are putting other people out when you would still like to be of service.

It is the time for humility and for faith that has been purified through lived experience.

Old age is not the road to death, but the path to life; fullness of life at last, and 'divinised' in Christ forever. But the difficult transformation must be accepted – the passage to that other life – just as the grain of wheat must die in the ground before it produces the ear of corn.

For the elderly person, the time is past for running towards others, but not for living in Christ as he lives in us. This is essential if the fruit is to mature.

I'm growing old, Lord,
   and growing old is hard!
I can't run any longer,
   I can't even walk fast.
I can no longer carry heavy weights
   or go upstairs quickly.
My hands have started to tremble
   and my eyes tire rapidly
   as they go through the pages of my book.
My memory is failing and obstinately hides
   dates and names
   that it knows quite well.

I'm growing old, and the links of affection,
   established over many long years,
   become slack, one by one,
   and sometimes they break.
So many of the people I know,
so many of the people I love,
go away and disappear
   into the distance
that my first glance at the daily newspaper
   becomes an anxious search through the death
   notices.

I find myself alone, Lord,
   a little more alone every day,
alone with my memories
   and with past sorrows

that always remain
very much alive in my heart,
while many of the joys
seem to have taken flight.

Understand me, Lord!
You who burned up your existence
in thirty-three intense years,
you don't know what it's like to be growing old slowly
and to be there
while life escapes implacably
from this poor rusted body,
an old machine with grinding gears,
a machine that doesn't work;
and above all, to be there
waiting,
waiting for the time to pass,
time that passes so slowly on certain days
that it seems to be mocking me as it turns and drags,
before me,
around me,
refusing to yield to the approaching night
and finally allowing me … to sleep.

How can one believe, Lord, that time today
is the same as time long ago,
time that went so fast on certain days,
certain months,
so fast that I couldn't catch it

and it got away from me
before I was able to fill it with life?

Today I have time, Lord,
too much time,
time piling up beside me,
unused,
and I'm there, motionless,
    and no good for anything.

I'm growing old, Lord,
    and growing old is hard,
so hard that some of my friends
    often ask for this life to be ended,
    a life which seems to them
    to be of no use from now on.

They're wrong, my child, says the Lord,
and you're wrong too.
    Perhaps you don't say what they are saying,
    but sometimes you agree with them.
All your brothers and sisters
    need you,
and I need you today,
    as I needed you yesterday.
Because a beating heart, though it may be worn out,
    still gives life
    to the body it inhabits,
and the love in this heart can gush forth,

often stronger and purer,
when the tired body finally leaves space for it.
Some very full lives,
    you see,
    can be empty of love,
    while others,
    seemingly very ordinary,
    radiate love infinitely.

Look at my mother, Mary,
    weeping,
    motionless at the foot of my cross.
She was there,
standing upright, certainly,
    but she too was powerless,
tragically *powerless*.

She did nothing,
    she was simply there,
completely collected,
completely welcoming,
offering herself completely,
    and in this way, with me,
    she saved the world,
    giving back to it
    all the love that men and women had lost
    along the pathways of time.

Today, with her,
    standing by the crosses of the world,
    you must gather the enormous suffering of humanity,
    dead wood to be burned in the fire of love.
But welcome the efforts and the joys also,
because gathered flowers are lovely,
    but they are of no use
    unless they are given to somebody,
    and so many people think about living
    but forget to give.

Believe me,
    your life today
    can be richer than it was yesterday
if you accept growing old,
    if you accept being a motionless sentinel watching
    for the evening;
and if you suffer because you have nothing in your
    hands that you can give,
then offer your powerlessness,
and together, I tell you,
we will continue saving the world.

Pathways of Prayer

At the bar of friendship

We are like bottles of vintage wine. We are valuable, but if we're shaken we lose our value. We must allow our hearts to lie still so that our wine can be good, comforting those who come to drink in friendship.

With Open Heart

Reasons to live

She's twenty years old and normally bursting with health, but she's exhausted. Lately she's been sleeping in very late and getting up feeling tired. She drags herself round from armchair to armchair. She's in the grips of a mysterious tiredness.

He is known for his laziness. However, for the last three months he's been getting up every night to work. He only sleeps for a few hours. He's in love and planning to go away with the object of his affections. He's in fine form. Love has awakened extraordinary energies in him that he himself didn't think he was capable of.

Chronically exhausted people seem to be more common these days. It's not a healthy tired feeling, the kind you get after a hard day's work or some vigorous exercise. It's more like having the air knocked out of you, like a boxer at the losing end of a match. It's exhaustion brought on by the stress of modern living and the eternal chase after 'happiness'. Bits of your life get lost. You are physically debilitated by stress and your life inevitably breaks up into little pieces.

People must be given reasons to live, reasons good enough to motivate them into picking up the pieces, sealing up the cracks, regaining their vitality and living again.

With Open Heart

My friend died last night, Lord

*I*t is God's will that each of his children is born, lives *and dies. But we should all die a 'natural' death at the end of our lives. Premature deaths from accidents or illness are not God's doing, nor are they 'the will of God' any more than just a matter of luck.*

Most accidents are the sad consequences of our freedom. It is only with the help of the Spirit that we can discover the extent of our own responsibility, as well as that of our brothers and sisters, in the dovetailing of all that we do. Many 'accidents' would be avoided if we lived as Jesus asked us to live.

Many illnesses are still incurable because we haven't yet succeeded in harnessing nature. This is our task as human beings. God gave us the earth to subdue and to put at the service of humankind, and he trusts us. With some exceptions, he doesn't take over from us by performing 'miracles'. It is up to scientists, researchers and doctors to continue the struggle. We cause many of our own illnesses by not using our bodies properly and by not paying attention to what they are saying to us. All too often we devote a lot more money, intelligence and energy to inventing ways of killing each other than to finding and exploiting ways to protect life and bring it to its full potential.

Fortunately, God does not abandon us; he has come in Jesus Christ to be with us in our struggle throughout our lives. The all-powerful gift of his love is with us always, and our suffering, while not a good thing in itself, can help to make us even more aware of Jesus Christ's saving love.

My friend died last night, Lord,
    his life
    ebbing away,
fighting the cancer to the very end,
with his family and a caring medical team.

I'm not saying, Lord:
since this is what you wanted,
may your will be done;
and still less am I saying: may your holy will be done.
    But I'm telling you, very quietly,
    very quietly, because so many people
    will never understand,
I'm telling you, Lord, that my friend died…
    and you could do nothing about it;
you couldn't do what I so desperately longed for,
you couldn't do what I so foolishly hoped for.
    And I'm weeping,
    torn apart,
    shattered,
    but my heart is at peace

because this morning, I understood a little better
    that you were weeping with me.
Yes, Lord, I understood...
    thanks to you,
    and thanks to my friends;
but help me to believe
    that you want life,
    not death,
    and that because you love more
you suffer more than any of us
    when you see so many of your children
    dying before their time.

    Apart from a few exceptions,
    and this is your mystery,
I understood that because of your respect and love
    for us
you never wanted to take our place
in the battle against illness,
    but always offered to suffer with us
    and to struggle with us.

    I understood...
because my friend, Lord,
instead of asking you for a miracle
asked you to give his medical team
    the strength to search
    and to struggle till the end in their efforts to find
    a cure.

For himself,
   he implored you to give him the courage to suffer,
to accept the two operations,
the treatments and all the pain,
so that others after him
might suffer less
and even be cured someday.

   For his family and friends
   he didn't ask for the grace of resignation
but for the grace to stand up for life,
   to respect it,
   to develop it,
and until the very end, lulled by the music he loved,
   he asked for everyone...
   the joy of living.

Lord, my friend didn't offer up his suffering
because he used to say that suffering is evil
and God doesn't like suffering.
He offered his long and painful battle
   against suffering;
   this prodigious energy,
   the strength he showed
   thanks to you, Lord,
the superabundance of love and faith he needed
   so as not to despair,

but to believe that this life
is restored through you, beyond death.

My friend, Lord,
didn't give his suffering,
 but like you,
 with you,
 oh my Saviour Jesus,
 he gave his life
 that we might live.

My friend died last night, Lord,
 and I am weeping,
 but my heart is at peace
because my friend died last night,
 but with you,
 he gave me life.

Pathways of Prayer

Often I am quiet

A gaping void exists in people that nothing can fill.
If they decide to live in truth, going from hunger
to hunger, from thirst to thirst, one day they will
reach a sunny glade where life awaits them and their
emptiness will be filled. But they must first experience
several deaths. They must not sit idly on the side of
the road or lose their way on dead-ends.

Often when I'm talking with people who tell me
about their problems, I feel that they're unconsciously
looking for some sort of fulfilment or nourishment
beyond what they're struggling for. I say nothing;
whether it is out of respect, timidity or lack of faith,
I don't know. I should probably speak up, for I am a
disciple of Christ, who said that he came to give us
life and to give it to us in abundance. Since no one
else will remind them of this, perhaps I should.

With Open Heart

The longest hours

He works on an assembly line. He explains that the hours aren't the same length. The first one is sixty minutes long; the second longer; the third even longer; and the last one just goes on and on endlessly. The last ten minutes are eternal, but to gain a little overtime pay, the workers start the line up again. It's dangerous, but they all do it. He does it too. Suddenly, the other day, he realised how alienated he had become. 'I told myself that our devotion to the assembly line equals our love for the Lord.' That same evening he explained how the requirements of the assembly line even dominated the love lives of the workers. On certain days, one was too exhausted even to make love.

More than 10,000 workers near where I live work on assembly lines, on day shifts and night shifts. For them, some men have reinvented slavery, while others are surprised that they're still fighting for shorter working hours and longer paid holidays. As for me, I continue driving around in the car they built for me.

Continue driving, my friend, but preach the fight for justice and never forget that your car is a gift from your brothers. You'll never quite repay them your debt of love.

With Open Heart

If each note said...

If each note of music were to say: one note does not
   make a symphony,
   there would be no symphony.
If each word were to say: one word does not make a book,
   there would be no book.
If each brick were to say: one brick does not make a wall,
   there would be no house.
If each drop of water were to say: one drop does not make
   an ocean,
   there would be no ocean.
If each seed were to say: one grain does not make a field
   of corn,
   there would be no harvest.
If each one of us were to say: one act of love cannot save
   mankind,
   there would never be justice and peace on earth.

   The symphony needs each note.
   The book needs each word.
   The house needs each brick.
   The ocean needs each drop of water.
   The harvest needs each grain of wheat.
   The whole of humanity needs you
      as and where you are.
         You are unique.
   No one can take your place.

The Breath of Love

To struggle is to be Christian

Struggle is an integral part of being human. We grow in and through struggle.

A baby struggles to physically separate from its mother.

A child struggles to be special in his parents' eyes.

An adolescent and a teenager struggle to become independent, then freely rejoin the family and society.

Couples struggle to retain their individuality within their marriage.

Groups struggle collectively to defend human rights and develop their identity.

Society struggles to obtain or defend its right to wealth, power and knowledge.

Without these struggles, human beings cannot grow to become what they are – creators of themselves and, with others, creators of humanity.

At the heart of these struggles we unite with God, who works constantly to 'make' men and women and all humanity. Let us make them in our image.

In this context, struggle is Christian; it is the absence of struggle that is unchristian.

With Open Heart

No room for discouragement

Everything is going badly for you. Your life is one long series of regrets. Nothing seems worthwhile to you any more. You have given up trying: *What's the point? I'll never be able to solve my problems; there's no hope.* Discouragement has completely paralysed you. You refuse to fight back any more. You no longer have the upper hand – you're just living your life out now without purpose or hope. If you're discouraged, it's because you put all your trust in your own efforts and now you realise that you can't go it alone. Had you placed your trust in God, you would still feel regret for your failings but you wouldn't be discouraged. You forget that God is as loving and as all-powerful after you've fallen as before. Discouragement is clear proof that you've placed too much confidence in yourself and too little in God.

Don't try to gloss over your failings and sins: *If only I could have prevented that; If only I could go back; If only I could start all over again; I can't understand why I should have so many problems; It's not fair; It's just my nature, so what can I do about it?* If you really want to overcome sin, you first have to recognise that you are a sinner. Don't try to cover it up. Don't look for excuses or try to forget about it or deny it, for if you do, you're closing the door to the truth about yourself. Learn to accept your failures, your difficulties, your habits of sin – those occasions of sin that you cannot escape.

Jesus Christ has not come to take away all our temptations or to eliminate the possibility of sin. Rather, he has come to take away the sins of the world. The saints themselves were not exempt from the struggle against evil. St Paul in his Epistle to the Romans underlines this fact: 'For I do not understand what I do, for it is not what I wish that I do, but what I hate, that I do... For I do not the good that I wish, but the evil that I do not wish, that I perform... For I am delighted with the law of God according to the inner person, but I see another law in my members, warring against the law of my mind and making me prisoner to the law of sin that is in my members. Unhappy person that I am: Who will deliver me from the body of this death?'

In the eyes of God, a person's real value is not measured by the ineffectual nature of their temptations or the infrequency of their falls, or even the absence of materially grave sin, but rather, first and foremost, by their complete confidence in their all-powerful Saviour, by their love and by their determination to keep trying in spite of failures. As long as traces of discouragement and melancholy persist in your attitude to yourself and your world, you do not yet trust completely in the compassion and forgiveness of the Lord, for the thought of his mercy should fill you with peace and joy.

When the prodigal son returned home, his father wanted nothing more than that the past be forgotten. He ordered a feast so that all might rejoice with him. 'There is more joy in heaven over one sinner who repents than over ninety-nine just who have no need of repentance.' Jesus Christ hates sin, but he generously and even lavishly shows pity to the sinner. If you have sinned, the Lord comes to you to show you his love and to offer you his redemptive mercy: the incomprehensible mystery of God's love for man. All things work together unto good for those who love God, even sin. Each fall is a sign, an invitation, to offer yourself to your Saviour.

You know your own weaknesses only too well. You see yourself at the mercy of every onslaught of temptation. Your egocentricity and selfishness seem to be gaining the upper hand rather than decreasing. You are even more acutely aware now of your failure to love. Don't give way to discouragement, but rather, rejoice, for the Lord came to save sinners and not the just. If you surrender yourself to him, he will forgive you and lead you to salvation. How can you ask for forgiveness if you do not see the evil that is present in your life? Why should you come to Jesus Christ in search of salvation if you experience no need for salvation? You will not find peace of mind through greater self-assurance or through a misplaced trust in your own virtue. This kind of peace of mind is pure illusion, for it implies that you no longer have any need for Jesus Christ, and you will find yourself alone, terribly alone and terribly vulnerable, without him. 'I have not come to save the just, but the sinner.' 'I have come to save what was lost.' 'It's not those who are well who have need of the physician, but those who are sick.'

Be particularly wary of the type of discouragement that can arise out of sins against purity. Sins of this kind can create a feeling of emptiness and malaise, which, coupled with a fear of having become the slave of instinct, can lead you to exaggerate your actual situation. Sins of weakness are not as serious as sins against faith, hope and love. A habit of sin restricts the exercise of your freedom, but be patient. You shouldn't be discouraged by your own weakness if you also recognise that God's grace is sufficient for you. The grace of God will never fail you, but you have to open yourself to receive it. There are two perversions of the Christian moral life that have to be guarded against: staying down once you've fallen and sitting by the side of the road thinking that you've already reached your destination. Your failings should make you recognise your own weakness. They will help you to become a little child again and to place your hand in the Father's as you make your way to your eternal destination.

'I keep the Lord always within my sight; for he is at my right hand, I shall not be moved. For this reason my heart is glad and my soul rejoices; moreover my body also will rest secure.'

The Christian Response

SECTION 2

TO LIVE THE GOSPEL

Prayer is saying to God...

Praying is going forward to meet our Father, God-Love. Prayer is saying to God:

'Source, give me living water
          flowing between the banks of my everyday life.
          Without you, I would become stagnant water
          and die.

Sun,   give me light
          shining on my way today and tomorrow.
          Without you, I would live in darkness and
          be lost.

Wind,   fill my sails
          – they are hoisted to receive you.
          Without you, I would never leave the harbour.

Breeze, I am waiting for your breath
          to carry me on my fight.
          Without you, I would be a bird with polluted
          feathers.

Artist,   touch me with your bow
          and draw music from my strings and
          my wood.

Without you, I would remain forever silent
in my case.

God,   great Artist, I am here, receptive
as a violin held in your loving arms,
waiting for you to play me.
I offer myself to you as your bride
– embrace me in your Love
and our child will be
music that will make the world sing with joy.'

'Yes, you must pray, for prayer is
    going out to meet God, who is coming to
    meet us,
    knowing that he is our Life and our Love,
    being totally composed
    and offering ourselves totally
        to be loved even before we love
        others.'

Lord, deliver me from myself

There are men and women who are their own victims, more miserable than you can imagine because they are condemned to loving no one but themselves. You must understand their suffering to free them, for this suffering is nothing less than a living hell. If they find a friend who makes them realise that they are their own tormentors, it is the first step in their salvation, especially if they find a committed Christian who is to them the light and joy that can draw them away from themselves.

Perhaps then they will pray, 'Lord, deliver me from myself.' If they ask this earnestly, it is the first step on the road to salvation.

We too can say this prayer every night when we come home to escape men and women and God.

Lord, do you hear me?

I'm suffering dreadfully,
locked in myself,
prisoner of myself.
I hear nothing but my voice,
I see nothing but myself
and behind me there is nothing but suffering.

Lord, do you hear me?

Deliver me from my body; it is nothing but hunger, with its thousands of tentacles outstretched to appease its insatiable appetite.

Lord, do you hear me?

Deliver me from my heart; when I think that it's overflowing with love, I realise angrily that it is again myself that I love more than the loved one.

Lord, do you hear me?

Deliver me from my mind; it is full of itself, of its ideas, its opinions; it cannot carry on a dialogue, as no words reach it but its own.

Alone, I am bored,
I am weary,
I hate myself,
I am disgusted with myself.
For ages I have been turning around inside myself like a sick man in his feverish bed.

Everything seems dark, ugly, horrible.
It's because I can look only through myself.
I feel ready to hate people and the whole world.
It's because I'm disappointed that I cannot love them.
I would like to get away,
walk, run, to another land.

I know that joy exists; I have seen it on singing faces.
I know that light exists; I have seen it in radiant eyes.
But Lord, I cannot get away, for I love my prison and
I hate it,
for my prison is myself
and I love myself, Lord.
I both love and loathe myself.

Lord, I can no longer find my own door.
I grope around blindly,
I knock against my own walls, my own boundaries.
I hurt myself,
I am in pain.
I am in too much pain and no one knows it, for no one
has come in.
I am alone, all alone.

Lord, Lord, do you hear me?
Lord, show me my door,
    take me by the hand.
Open the door.
Show me the way,
the path leading to joy, to light.

But Lord, do you hear me?

My child, I have heard you.
I am sorry for you.

I have long been watching your closed shutters. Open them; my light will come in.
I have long been standing at your locked door. Open it; you will find me on the threshold.
I am waiting for you, the others are waiting for you, but you must open up.
You must come out.

Why choose to be a prisoner of yourself?
You are free.
It is not I who locked the door,
it is not I who can open it.
For it is you, from the inside, who persist in keeping it solidly barred.

Prayers of Life

Lord, I would like to be sure that you are with me in the struggle

M any Christians are committed to being actively involved in the Church. They are needed more than ever. Others are committed to works of charity. They are needed too – those who have been hurt need good Samaritans. But far fewer are committed to working in trade unions or in politics. People distrust them and some even condemn them if they don't share their opinions.

Dom Hélder Câmara says with a smile, 'When I'm concerned about the poor, they say I'm a saint. When I denounce the structures that make people poor, they say I'm a communist.'

It is praiseworthy to comfort the victims, but even more praiseworthy to fight against the 'sinful structures' spoken of by Pope John Paul II. These structures produce the victims and they threaten peace. Fighting against them is the social dimension of charity.

The worlds of economics, social order and politics are certainly tough and the struggle that takes place in them is sometimes violent. Christians can be frightened by this. But not all violence is to be condemned. Parents who fight to defend a child from danger are 'violent', but their violence comes from

love. The Church has never condemned 'defensive'
war and doesn't condemn people who rise up against
oppression. Hatred does not come from God.

Christians should not be shirkers who leave their
brothers and sisters to dirty their hands in struggles
that are both just and necessary.

Lord,
I fight, together with my comrades,
   loyal to my movement
   and to my organisation,
united in the struggle
for a life that is more just and more human.
But the battle is hard
   and very often I'm afraid
   of being in it without you.

  Lord,
I'd like to be sure that you're with me in the struggle.
Alas, people are needed to stand up for the cause
   when a war is raging.
Perhaps all of them will retire one day,
   refusing to become involved,
   but that won't happen tomorrow.
   And today
   there are many causes to defend
   and there are wars

to mobilise the combatants.
People are needed to care for the wounded
and to bury the dead,
    because the victims are legion
    and they call on us to look after them.
People are needed to sign the treaties
    when some battles are over.
But many more people are needed
    to avoid wars by building peace,
    the peace that flourishes
    when justice reigns.

I hesitated for a long time
before becoming involved in this peaceful struggle.
Along with some of the other shirkers, I calmed my
conscience,
    holding forth learnedly
    that one person alone
    cannot lift up the world.
I kept away from suspect groups
    of the revolutionary type.
I thought that the worlds of economics,
    trade unions,
    politics
    were polluted worlds
and I was afraid that plunging into them would mean
dirtying my hands.
But I wasn't at peace, Lord.

And weren't you there,
    challenging me constantly
    through what was going on around me?
For you have told me that I must love my brothers and
sisters.
But loving them
is not only offering them a smile
    or holding out a hand.
If they have nothing to eat,
if they are ignorant and exploited
    and above all if they are deprived
    of bread, of dignity,
can I send them back home
    with my hand closed on my money,
    saying to them:
    'I love you'
    or even:
    'I'm praying for you!'

I became involved but you know it's hard,
because while those who struggle
    and serve
    amid the ravages of war
    are admired and decorated,
those who struggle to change this unjust and cruel
world
    into a world of peace and harmony
    are often criticised
    and sometimes judged severely.

You pushed me into it, Lord,
so I ask you not to leave me alone,
because when I become very involved
I find myself in the thick of the struggle,
attacked...
    with blows raining down
    from adversaries
    and sometimes from friends;
misjudged...
    I'm considered too right wing,
    too left wing,
    too much to the centre
    and everyone paints me in a different colour.
I search, and I search for myself,
and I have doubts sometimes.

Because the struggle is not straightforward
and I suffer as a result.
And the battles are so tough
    that I often lose sight of you,
    I admit it.
    Alone
    in the evening,
    before you,
    I regret this.
    I'm ashamed of it
    and I ask for your forgiveness.

Because if I want to struggle,
I want you to be with me.

Hear my prayer, Lord,
   for I know
   that our human constructions
   are not the Kingdom.
I know also that the yeast
needs the dough to make it rise.
   And the dough needs flour,
   and the flour needs wheat,
   and the wheat, the flour and the dough
require the work of our hands
   so that the bread may be baked
   and justly shared out,
   and so that from this bread that is offered
   you may make your Eucharist.

   Lord,
give me, I pray,
the yeast of your love!

Help me not to judge and condemn
the people who sit calmly on the sidelines,
   discussing,
   watching us as we battle in the arena.
And take away the jealously I feel
   when I see them

profiting without a qualm from our victories,
    forgetting that they owe them to us.
Help me to understand,
to accept,
    that people of the same faith
    profess ideas
    that are opposed to mine;
let me be able to receive communion at the same table
      with those who are on the other side in the fight.

Let loyalty to my movement,
    to my party,
    never be an absolute for me;
for me, whose involvement in the struggle is a matter
of conscience,
    who while accepting its instructions
    and obeying faithfully
frequently rebels
when your Church speaks
    and sometimes refuses to follow its directives.
Give me the strength,
    the strength to say no
when my conscience refuses to say yes,
    and the courage to accept
    the reproaches of friends
    who accuse me of treason,
    even though for me it is a matter
    of true loyalty.

Help me to know your Gospel,
not to look for prescriptions
that can't be found in it,
     but to be nourished by your Word
so that this good seed
may sprout from my well-prepared ground,
may bloom as good news for my brothers and sisters
and may ripen for them
as fruits of justice and peace.

Finally, Lord, grant me
     that supreme grace,
     the grace that only you can give,
     to love my adversaries
     as well as my allies,
not only in the secret temple
of my better feelings,
     but by listening to them,
     respecting them,
     trying to understand them;
     and the grace to believe
     that sincerity
     and generosity
     are not reserved for me,
but can be found in others,
     even if they are enemies.
For you know how I get carried away, Lord,
and how I tend, too quickly perhaps,
to refer to this as my passion for justice!

Sometimes I am so anxious to get my own back
and to hurt
those who have hurt me
that I find it hard,
yes, very hard to forgive.

Lord, give me the strength to forgive.

I am with you, says the Lord,
I am with you in your struggles,
because I am with all those who fight
    to defend their brothers and sisters,
    even when they venture onto battlegrounds
    far from the protected enclosure
    where the fearful lie dormant.
But look at what is going on in your heart, my child,
    because I cannot be present
    where there is hatred
and only love can ensure your victory
    while at the same time ensuring mine.
Why do you doubt, you of little faith?
    Happy are you!
    Happy are all of you
    who have the courage to risk
    getting your hands and your feet dirty
    in the struggle for justice,
because I didn't come

for those who stayed clean
   by remaining seated
   with their hands in their pockets.

Don't be afraid of anything!
I washed the feet of my disciples,
and if the feet of the combatants
are covered in dust,
   I'll wash them too.

Pathways of Prayer

Why are you hidden, Lord?

The silence of God weighs on us like a dead weight.
Even today I listened to the bitter complaints of
some people who feel this weight. I understand how
they feel because I often feel that way myself. This
evening, in the face of their suffering, I also suffer.

Why are you hidden, Lord?
Why do you hide in this grey day, where my work
    weighs on me like a punishment?
Why do you hide in my untidy house, where
    everything has to be put into place daily?
Why do you hide in our worn-out love
    like stagnant water whose source has dried up?
Why do you hide in this body that calls to me,
    flesh wanting my own hungry flesh?
Why do you hide in the sickness of my body,
    faithful, suffering, unwanted spouse?
Why do you hide in my human struggles
    when I am fighting with and for my brothers
    and sisters?
Why do you remain hidden, you who came to this
    earth,
    you who spoke so forcefully,
    you who wept so piteously?

Why do you hide in the night – my obsession –
   the night that falls after sundown,
   the night flowing in my heart like approaching
   death?
Why do you hide, Lord, why?
Speak to me, Lord!
Dear Lord, why do you hide when I know that you
   are there?

With Open Heart

Life is before me, Lord, but you are with me on the journey

Many young people are afraid of the future. They are particularly worried about their professional future and about their future family life. They don't know what paths to choose and they don't know where these paths will take them. Some become very anxious and avoid making a choice by refusing to grow up. Fear is unhealthy. It paralyses. The greatness of human beings lies in our capacity to take risks in our lives – after careful reflection, of course – but without expecting the kind of 'all risks insurance' that is not to be found.

Yes, risk-taking is dangerous. Committing ourselves consciously and loyally to Jesus Christ does not save us from effort, but it does guarantee peace. He wants us to be truly happy and he wants to help us to attain this happiness regardless of the difficulties we meet on our path through life.

Life is before me, Lord,
   like an enticing fruit;
but life often frightens me,
   because if I want to gather its fruits
   I must leave home
   and start my journey;

I must walk,
and keep on walking,
on a road that turns and returns endlessly,
on which I can't see ahead
    the landscape of the future
    or the hidden obstacles,
    the hands stretched out towards me
    or the faces turned away.

Setting out, Lord,
is a thrilling adventure.
I want to live...
but often I'm afraid.

I'm afraid of entering the huge building site
tomorrow, where the crowds of world builders go
about their business.
    Will I find a job there?
    So many new hands are left without work
    and so many heads bursting with ideas
    are waiting for employment!

I'm afraid of this mysterious world
    that fascinates and terrifies me,
    because I hear the shouts of laughter
    and I see the pleasures
    that beckon to me from afar,
but I also hear
the clamour of human suffering,

cries that arouse my indignation,
cries that I cannot silence.

I'm afraid of this love,
    which I desire with all my being,
    at the dawn of my days
    and in the depth of my nights.
Mysterious energy that inundates my heart
    and overflows my body,
and with lengthening days, persistent longing
    to encounter a face,
to recognise and be recognised
    as the one uniquely sought.
Hunger to caress it with a glance,
    to encircle it with my hands,
to taste its lips at last and let my own be tasted.
Hunger already, that this love
    may through us become flesh
    and cry out,
    the cry of new life
    when love bears fruit.

I desire, but at the same time I'm afraid, Lord.
So many efforts to love have miscarried before my
eyes,
    illusions of happiness
    like bubbles that have burst.
So many loves are tested
    and not risked in the end.

So many couples among my friends
    who believed they were united forever
    and then broke up their relationship quickly!

Yes, I'm afraid, Lord.
    I dare to admit it
    and I dare to say it to you.
But if I close my eyes today
it is not because I refuse
to see the road ahead of me,
    but in order to find you, to pray to you.
    Because I want to live, Lord,
    I want to live,
and I trust you.

    Oh my God,
let me never forget to thank you for life,
    because life is yours,
    you who are the Father,
    the Father of all life,
you who have made me your child,
    your child born for joy.

Make me proud to be human,
    standing up straight as men and women are called
    to stand,
accepting from you this marvellous vocation
    to create myself,
    to raise myself, to grow

so as to set out rich and free
  on the road that lies ahead.

Let me welcome life
  wholeheartedly,
  firmly,
because my parents transmitted it to me through love,
  even if the love
  perhaps
  was fragile,
and I am responsible for my life
  because they gave it to me.

Help me not to waste my life,
  life of a body that overstretches itself
  and of a soul that is losing its way;
never to steal life from others,
  but always to welcome it
  when it is offered;
never to lock it up and keep it in my own heart
  instead of sharing it
  with my brothers and sisters
  who need it so much.

Give me the desire to seek you always
  so that I may meet you, know you and love you
  and become with you the friend you desire,
welcoming your life in my life
  so that my flowers and my fruit

may be yours and mine
at the same time.

Help me to go forward
    without wanting to know
    what I'm going to find
    at every bend on the road,
not with my head in the clouds
    but with my feet on the ground
    and my hand in yours.

I'll leave home then, Lord,
    confidently, joyfully,
and I'll set out fearlessly on the unknown road:
    the journey of life is before me,
but you are travelling with me.

Pathways of Prayer

Father be praised!

We praise you, Father, for the sea, the sky and the stars.
We praise you for the power of the atom.
We praise you for the oil flowing like rivers,
      for the rockets like lightning among the stars,
      for the satellites hovering over the planets.
We praise you, Father, for science and technology.
We praise you for the matter that you have created,
      which, though it seems dead to our eyes,
      is yet living matter,
      matter transformed,
the meeting place of divine action and human activity.

We praise you, Father, for the artists and technicians,
      for the scholars and the countless workers
      who take that matter and use it and transform it.
We praise you for the eternal plan of your love,
      which governs that great movement forward of the
      universe.

We praise you for your Son.
Through him all things came to be, and not one thing
has its being but through him.
Through him, you continue to create all things,
      to make them holy,
      to give them life,
      to bless them and to give them to us.

It is by him, and with him, and in him,
    God the Father almighty,
    and in the unity of the Holy Spirit,
that we honour and glorify you,
    for ever and ever.

Lord, let me be the one who, from time to time,
    in the still of the night,
looks with the eyes of a son upon what you
have created
    so that I may praise the Creator.
Let me be as an excited child before the Father
    so that he may smile down upon the child that
    I am.

Meet Christ and Live

Lord, pardon my error

Lord, forgive the ignorance and the fear of those who
try to hide in sacristies, convents and churches.
    But forgive me, too,
        because I know that you are with us and among us and
        I often forget it.

Lord, why must we always be looking at the surface of
things and events that we do not understand?
    And why can't I receive your Light
        in such a way that it illuminates the whole world
        and every step of my way?
Why can't I be the 'seer' who discovers you, hidden
and needy, among us?
Why can't I be one of those who gather the blossoms
of the gospel in the evening and present them to you?

Lord, make me understand
    that I must not run away from the world,
since you are waiting for me in the world;
    that there is no need for me to put you in contact
    with life,
since you are already present among men and women,
who are my brothers and sisters;
    that far from fleeing the active life,
    I should join in your action among all people.

Grant, Lord, not that I may see the obstacles to your coming into the world, but above all that I may know
   where to meet you,
   how to recognise your signs
   and your invitations.
And if, some day, I speak your name, let it not be to speak of a distant, inaccessible, unknown and unknowable God,
but to introduce you as my friend, Lord,
   as my companion-in-arms,
   and of course as a transcendent God,
   but as God present and acting in the world.

For you have risen, Lord, and your Holy Spirit is at work in human history
   to increase your whole body,
   to build the kingdom of the Father,
   to construct your Church.

'There is one among you whom you do not know.'
   I'm sorry, Lord, I didn't know it was you.
'The kingdom of God is among you.'
   Forgive me, Lord. I had forgotten.
'I am with you always; yea, to the end of time.'
      Again, Lord, I'm sorry. I've behaved as though
      I was alone in our Father's vineyard.

Meet Christ and Live

You could have, Lord

'Lord, you could have made us trees in a forest or sheep in
a flock.
You could have made us puppets dancing while you
pulled the strings.
   But you created us human, responsible and free –
   sons and daughters free to love you, sisters and
   brothers free to love each other.
      We thank you for that freedom, Lord!

Lord, you could have offered us a finished world –
   its roads constructed, its rivers bridged, its cities
   built and its factories full of docile workers
   producing perfect goods.
   But you created us human, responsible and free
   and we have the task of building up this world.
      We thank you for that freedom, Lord!

Lord, you could have arranged our marriages and
given us our families.
By imposing your will on us, you could have kept us
   together in permanent wedlock, peace and love.
You could have counted our kisses, regulated our
embraces and controlled our friendships.
   But you created us human, responsible and free –
   not dolls made of human flesh to be held in your arms,

but loved human children richly endowed with life
and free to love you or to refuse your love.

We thank you for that freedom, Lord!

But Lord, sometimes we behave badly and forget you,
our Father.

We destroy what you have created for us in our fragile
world and take for ourselves what you gave to others.

We struggle for power and exploit, injure and kill one
another.

Lord, you could have ceased to trust and love us and
withdrawn the power you gave us.

You could then have taken our place and made a heaven
on earth.

But you wanted us to remain human, responsible
and free!

So Lord, you sent us your Son, who was human,
responsible and free,

to love us and save us without taking back our
freedom.

And, Lord Jesus, you could have changed stones into
bread and fed those among us who are dying of
hunger.

You could have exerted your power and made us obey
you.

But you wanted us to remain human, responsible
and free!

Lord Jesus, you could have conquered your enemies and
given us peace.
You could then have reached your Father's heaven by a
different way, not the way of the cross.
  We would then have remained human and responsible,
  but we would have remained alone
  with our sins and our guilt,
  all that is left of love when it fails.

But Lord Jesus, you embraced our sins and our guilt
  when you embraced the dead wood of the cross
  and gave the tree new life and it bore new fruit.
  That fruit is saving Love that set us free.

Lord, I love you because you love me and want me to
be free.
I love you because you risked your glory for my
freedom.
I love you because you were omnipotent,
  but came to us without power,
  except for the power of Love.

Lord, I love you because the terrible freedom that causes
such suffering
  is also the wonderful freedom and that enables us
  to choose love.

So when we fall under the cross that we carry every
day
    or are angry about the cross borne by our fellow
men and women
    and curse God or simply sit with our eyes and ears
closed,
    give us the strength to stand up and go on our way
again,
        knowing that you will only help us to carry our cross
            if we carry it ourselves as you carried yours.

Breath of Love

Lord, I haven't yet made joy my own

Pleasure is relatively easy to obtain. It comes in many different forms and is connected mainly with the body. Like food, most pleasures are rapidly consumed and frequently leave us vaguely dissatisfied.

Joy is connected with the soul. It is not easily found. It is a virtue to be acquired, an incomprehensible mystery for those who haven't experienced it, and it can co-exist with the greatest suffering in the same heart.

Only God is perfect happiness, perfect joy. Only the pure of heart – in spite of their human limitations, in spite of the fact that during this life they can glimpse only a few reflections of the beauty and greatness of God, in spite of the pain of seeing their brothers and sisters suffering – can attain this joy by being open to God and receiving it from him. But isn't this the preserve of the saints? And as for us, can we say in all honesty that 'we have really made joy our own'?

I'm told, Lord, that one should smile,
   smile every day,
   and then smile again.

I'm told that joy is a solid Christian virtue
   and that a sad saint
   is a very sad saint.
I'm told that people can't bear witness to you
   unless their faces and their lives
   radiate your joy.
I want to believe this...
but I haven't yet
   made joy my own, Lord.

All too often joy is my faithless companion;
   it flies away,
   returns
   and flies off again.
Just when I think I've grasped it,
   it disappears,
and a few clouds
trail across the blue sky of my heart,
   and sometimes
   they explode into storms...
   it rained on my joy.

Lord,
   it's your fault
that I haven't yet made joy my own!
You've told me that men and women are my brothers
and sisters
   and that I should love all of them,
   even my enemies.

I've tried, I keep on trying, and sometimes I think I'm
succeeding.
    But then I've discovered, Lord,
    that to love
    means to be ready
    to share the suffering of those one loves
    … and often their suffering is colossal!

Lord,
I don't understand.
Is it possible to be completely happy
when into the recesses of peaceful days
    or into the silence of the night
comes the sound
    of cries that cannot be silenced:
    the murmuring of the unemployed,
    the moans of the starving,
the tears of separated spouses and dispersed children,
    the rattles of the dying,
    the shrieks of the tortured,
    the terrible din of battles…
atrocious concert of a thousand discords
that rises up to us,
endlessly,
from humanity torn apart,
    members scattered,
    members bleeding,
of a body that you willed to be united and happy.

Lord,
I don't understand.
    Your apostle Paul said:
    'If one part of the body suffers,
    all the other parts suffer with it'
    and I suffer a little,
and I know I would suffer more
if I loved more,
but I believe that I would stop suffering
if the cries of my brothers and sisters stopped.

    No, I couldn't be completely happy
when so many members of my family
    are unhappy.
But there are some who could, Lord.
As they watch television during a meal
and see pictures of disasters
that are shown every day,
    they say: 'Isn't that terrible!',
and then
after an awkward silence:
'What's for dessert today?'
When they open the newspaper
    and read the main headline they exclaim:
    'Another bombing attack and more innocent
    people killed.

    It's appalling!'
And then, a moment later:
    'There's a great film on TV on Sunday,
    we ought to watch it!'
At their important meetings, they announce:
    'What ought to be done is…
    if it hasn't been done already…'
They discuss the problem for two hours…
and then before going home they have a drink
together
    and laugh at each other's stories.
During the prayer of the faithful,
these good Christians pray regularly
    for all who suffer from any kind of poverty…
    and then proclaim in song the joy of being together,
    with you,
the joy of being able to offer your sacrifice to the
Father.
And they still say:
One must live well!
It's not a sin to be happy;
it's unhealthy to make oneself feel guilty,
and even more so to make others feel guilty;
I've contributed already!
You have to trust people!
Jesus has overcome death, he is risen!
    Let's sing, let's embrace each other, let's be happy!

They say...
They say...
   and I also say, Lord,
   and I also live,
   and I also laugh,
but there are days when I'm afraid
   that my joy may not be genuine,
   that it may be just a burst of laughter
   to block out the cries of men and women.
I'm afraid that my joy
   may spring thoughtlessly from a good conscience
   that is satisfied with a few gifts offered
   and a few good deeds done.
I'm afraid that my momentary joy may simply mean
that I'm asleep,
   that it may be an escape into golden dreams
   supported by the illusion of a deep faith.

...Lord, I haven't yet made joy my own!

Lord,
if I haven't yet made joy my own,
   that is also because
you made us too small
   for your joy, a joy that is too much for us.
How can we be completely happy
   when so many hungers
   torture our bodies and our minds,
   so many hungers that can only be appeased

but never satisfied?
How can we be completely happy
    when life mocks us
    with unattainable dreams dancing in front of us
    every morning
    but never realised when evening comes?
How can we be completely happy
    when a hand held,
    when lips joined in a kiss,
    scarcely touch the inviolate mystery
    of the person who is with us?
How can we be completely happy
    when your face,
    occasionally glimpsed in prayer,
    is hidden afterwards
in the night that is too long?

… Lord, I haven't yet made joy my own!

Accept your limitations, my child,
says the Lord;
    you are not God,
    you are not almighty,
but you are a member of my body,
    and each one of these members
    receives a few morsels of joy,
    like a nourishing mouthful of bread,
like a refreshing draught of wine.

Welcome them.
It is I who give them to you.

But it's true, my child,
    that even though
    I am alive,
    risen from the dead,
    for you and for all,
    I am also crucified
    every day in the members of my body.
My passion has not been accomplished
    while my brothers and sisters suffer
and while you suffer with me.
I've warned you
    that this is the lot of disciples.

    Don't be ashamed to suffer,
    but do what you have to do
    for your brothers and sisters,
    where you are,
    generously.
Then you will know peace,
    great peace,
my peace,
that I promised:
    'Peace is what I leave with you,
    it is my own peace that I give you.'
As for the joy that you seek:
    to attain complete joy, my child,

you may have to wait for the day
when I will say to you:
'Well done, good and faithful servant...
enter into the joy of your master'

(MATTHEW: 25–21).

Pathways of Prayer

Jesus is condemned to death

So it was, brothers and sisters, that when I came
to you and preached Christ's message to you, I did
so without any high pretensions to eloquence or to
philosophy. I had no thought of bringing you any
other knowledge than that of Jesus Christ, and of
him as crucified. It was with distrust of myself, full of
anxious fear, that I approached you; my preaching,
my message depended on no persuasive language
devised by human wisdom, but rather on the proof
I gave you of spiritual power; God's power, not the
wisdom of men or women, was to be the foundation
of your faith.

(1 CORINTHIANS 2: 1–5)

Lord, it's too late for you to be quiet, you have
spoken too much; you have fought too much.
You were not sensible, you know; you exaggerated, it
was bound to happen.
You called the better people a breed of vipers.
You told them that their hearts were black sepulchres
with fine exteriors.
You kissed the decaying lepers.
You spoke fearlessly with unacceptable strangers.
You ate with notorious sinners and you said that
street-walkers would be the first in Paradise.

You got on well with the poor, the tramps, the
crippled.
You belittled the religious regulations.
Your interpretation of the law reduced it to one little
commandment: to love.
Now they are avenging themselves.
They have taken steps against you: they have
approached the authorities and action will follow.

Lord, I know that if I try to live a little like you, I
shall be condemned.
I am afraid.
They are already singling me out.
Some smile at me, others laugh, some are shocked and
several of my friends are about to drop me.
I am afraid to stop.
I am afraid to listen to men's wisdom.
It whispers: you must go forward little by little,
everything can't be taken literally, it's better to come
to terms with the adversary...
And yet, Lord, I know that you are right.
Help me to fight.
Help me to speak.
Help me to live your Gospel
to the end,
to the folly of the Cross.

Prayers of Life

Jesus falls the third time

Again.
You do not move, for all the soldiers' beatings.
Lord, are you dead?
No, but utterly spent.
A minute of terrible anxiety.
But you begin again, just as you are, Lord, and walk
on. One step, then another...
Lord, you have fallen a third time, but this time close
to Calvary.

Again.
I fall every time.
I'll never get there.
But I've said that before, Lord, and please forgive me,
for you were right with me, you were just testing
my faith.
If I become discouraged, I am lost.
If I keep up the fight, I am saved.
For you fell a third time, but you had nearly reached
Calvary.

Prayers of Life

86

Too optimistic?

'You are too optimistic,' some readers will tell me. I won't defend myself against that charge. On the contrary, I'll thank those readers, for I see such an accusation as a compliment. Sometimes I am tempted to be pessimistic, but if I give in to temptation, I feel guilty about it.

I am indeed optimistic about the world today. Too optimistic? I don't think so. We are never too optimistic when we believe in the Risen Christ living his mystery at the very heart of the world. I think the gravest sin of Christians today is fear. Evil, sin, death – we must keep those things in mind, of course, but at the same time, we must see Christ victorious. Many people say, 'Everything is falling apart. A world is passing away.' But I say, 'A world is being born.' Death exists, but Jesus Christ has conquered death. Christ is alive!

Christ Is Alive

SECTION 3

TO HOPE IS TO BE OPEN

Lord, why did you tell me to love?

Those who have begun to give themselves to others are saved. In receiving their neighbour they will receive God and will be freed from themselves. We are our own worst enemy. At a human level we bring suffering on ourselves, and at a spiritual level we bar the road to God. There are people who are bent on refining themselves. They examine themselves, spend their time combating their faults and never get beyond themselves, except sometimes to cultivate little hothouse virtues cut to their own size. They are wrong. Certain teachers encourage them in this course, not realising that by pointing out such and such a fault to conquer, such and such a quality to acquire, they centre their attention on themselves and condemn them to stagnation. No – one should study people carefully to first find out not what is bad in them, but what is good in order to discover their potential. Next, study their environment in detail and help them to become an integral part of it by giving themselves to others.

Everyone can and must give themselves. If they have one talent, let them give that; if they have ten, let them give ten. It's only in giving that one can receive. But anyone who has begun this giving realises very quickly, if they are honest, that they can't retreat.

*They are afraid: one must then encourage them and
show them that it's only on the condition that they
give to others that they will succeed in their lives and
will know the joy of God.*

Lord, why did you tell me to love everyone?
I have tried, but I come back to you, frightened...
Lord, I was so peaceful at home, I was so comfortably
settled.
It was well furnished, and I felt cosy.
I was alone, I was at peace,
sheltered from the wind, the rain, the mud.
I would have stayed unsullied in my ivory tower.
But Lord, you have discovered a breach in my defences.
You have forced me to open my door.
Like a squall of rain in the face, the cry of other
people has awakened me;
like a gale of wind, a friendship has shaken me.
As a ray of light slips in unnoticed, your grace has
stirred me

... and, rashly enough, I left my door ajar. Now, Lord,
I am lost!
Outside, others were lying in wait for me.
I did not know they were so near; in this house, in
this street, in this office; my neighbour, my colleague,
my friend.

As soon as I began to open the door, I saw them, with out-stretched hands, burning eyes, longing hearts, like beggars on church steps.

The first ones came in, Lord. There was, after all, some space in my heart.
I welcomed them. I would have cared for them and caressed them, my very own little lambs, my little flock.
You would have been pleased, Lord. I would have served and honoured you in a proper, respectable way.
Till then, it was sensible...
But the next ones, Lord, the others, I had not seen them: they were hidden behind the first ones.
There were more of them and they were wretched; they overpowered me without warning.
We had to crowd in, I had to find room for them.

Now they have come from all over, in successive waves, pushing one another, jostling one another.
They have come from all over town, from all parts of the country, of the world; numberless, inexhaustible.
They don't come alone any longer but in groups, bound one to another.
They come bending under heavy loads; loads of injustice, of resentment and hate, of suffering and sin...
They drag the world behind them, with everything rusted, twisted or badly adjusted.

Lord, they hurt me! They are in the way, they are everywhere.
They are too hungry, they are consuming me!
I can't do anything anymore; as they come in, they push the door, and the door opens wider...
Lord, my door is wide open!
I can't stand it anymore! It's too much! It's no kind of life!
What about my job?
 my family?
 my peace?
 my liberty?
 and me?
Lord, I have lost everything. I don't belong to myself any longer; there's no more room for me at home.

Don't worry, God says, you have gained all.
While people came in to you,
I, your Father,
I, your God,
slipped in among them.

Prayers of Life

Lord, I have contemplated the faces of men and women at length

Men and women are body and spirit, in one. We believe that God created us 'in his image and likeness'. Thus it is whole human beings, body and soul, who are the images of God, and especially their faces – mysterious shop windows that display their innermost depths.

God spoke in the Old Testament, but nobody has ever seen God. Then one day, God took on a face. A face like ours, moulded from the same clay. In a certain sense, we can say from this point onwards that if God created us 'in his image and likeness', he himself, in his son Jesus, was created 'in the image and likeness' of men and women.

And another thing: through his love, Jesus Christ has incorporated all human beings into himself. As St Paul says, we have become members of his body. He gave us his life in our life, and we mustn't forget that our life is our souls and bodies together. We are brothers and sisters of Jesus Christ. We are members of the same family. It's not surprising, therefore, that we resemble each other. Jesus was a Jew, and it is not because of any particular features that we are like each other, but because of the family resemblance, that mysterious light that produces true beauty. We must develop this resemblance in ourselves and in

our brothers and sisters by being increasingly open,
through Jesus, to the life of God our Father. Then
we will change from being people with anonymous –
and sometimes even ill-formed – faces to people with
transfigured faces and eventually with resurrected
faces.

  The fact remains that from now on, the only face
that Jesus has on this earth is ours and that of our
brothers and sisters.

Lord, I have contemplated the faces of men and
women for a long time,
    and the eyes in the faces,
    and the look in the eyes,
speaking a language more profound than gestures and
words.
I turn back towards you, dazzled and overjoyed,
    but always more eager.

    Faces,
open books in which I have learned so much,
received so much from my brothers and sisters,
    my food,
    my nourishment,
unique faces, works of art,
    which no make-up,
    no faults,
    no wounds

could deform permanently
in the eyes of those who know how to look.
From what mysterious dough were you formed,
so that the breezes as well as the storms,
    the sunshine as well as the showers,
    of lives lived in the open air
    and also of very secret lives,
    are etched in your wrinkles?

Lord, I have admired
the architecture of faces,
    cathedrals,
    chapels
    or unobtrusive oratories,
and through the architecture I have known the riches
    and the poverty of the artist
    who fashioned them
    from the inside,
    from every one of his thoughts
    and from every one of his actions.

I have suffered terribly in the presence of faces that are
    damaged or deformed,
measuring the depth of sufferings that are hidden,
    like pain that sneaks up
    from nowhere.
I have seen some of these lost faces,
    adrift,
    drenched by thunderstorms,

while on others, alas,
I've been able to gather
    only a few tears
    that have escaped from the torrents locked away.

I've drunk long draughts
of the light from faces inhabited by the sun
    and my thirst has been quenched.
But I've waited a long time,
waited like one who watches for daybreak,
to see a smile on faces of night.
I've travelled the furrows
    on old faces,
    avenues or crevasses,
rediscovered traces
of the joys and sorrows
that have ploughed the earth of long human lives,
    and I turn back towards you,
    dazzled and overjoyed,
    but always eager.

    Why, Lord…
    Why am I so fascinated?
And why have I undertaken
these long pilgrimages
to the sanctuary of faces, so often?

I admit, Lord,
    that I began out of curiosity.

Books reveal so little about the mysteries of life;
    one must look further afield
    if one is to find the light.
I thought I might turn up hidden treasure
in this clay from which we are moulded,
    dust,
    living earth,
    inhabited;
    earth and spirit mingled
    to the point where one no longer knows
    where the earth is,
    where the spirit is,
    in these bodies and faces,
    so closely wedded to each other.

I was searching for life, Lord,
beyond the harmony of forms and colours.
I was searching for the 'person'
beyond all the personalities,
and beyond the persons I sought
... oh, unspeakable mystery!
    I was searching...
    and suddenly I found
that my hunger for faces was a hunger for God
    ... I was searching for you, Lord,
    and you were beckoning me!

    Lord, is it possible
that some believers

are still losing their way
even though they really want to meet you,
    and walking with their eyes in the clouds,
    unaware that they could see you every day
    when they meet their sisters and brothers on
    the road,
    because since you came among us,
    God, moulded from the same clay as ourselves,
God, who took on a face in Jesus our brother,
    nobody can meet other men and women
    without discovering something of you in them.

You, the child of Bethlehem,
    in the faces of smiling babies...
You, the chastiser of the Temple,
    in the faces of adolescents
    who don't know
    whether they are children or adults.
You, the one tempted in the desert,
    in the faces of people who are tormented,
    divided,
    torn apart
    by the evil always on offer.
You, transfigured,
    in the faces of men and women at prayer.
You, condemned and disfigured,
    in the faces of the tortured,
    groaning under blows,
    blows to the body,

blows to the heart.
You, risen from the dead,
    in the faces of those in whom love shines
    and has made its home
    as they sing the Easter Alleluia.

Lord,
    I want to keep going
on this unfinished pilgrimage,
seeking the faces of my brothers and sisters,
until that joyous day
when all will be in your light at last,
    and as I contemplate them
    I will be contemplating you.

But if I am to recognise you more easily
in the faces of my brothers and sisters,
    I must keep on travelling
    the long, hard road
    with you.

Help me, Lord,
to respect the faces,
    and never to de-face them
    by trying to seize
    fleeting beauties for myself,
or to gather from the surface of their living flesh
fruits that are ripening for others.

Let me never shut my eyes
　　to faces of a different colour,
　　to faces that are dark or repellent to me.
Let me never lose hope in my heart,
and let me never condemn
　　when pride,
　　egoism or hatred
have turned some faces
into grimacing masks for carnivals of death.

Give me the courage, Lord,
　　to search beneath the surface of the faces
　　and not to settle in attractive riverbanks
　　or in sad, unknown territory,
but on my pilgrimage to what lies beyond,
crossing over the frontiers of the visible,
　　let me return
　　to the bright Source of Light,
　　there in the calm lake of the heart,
where your image slowly takes shape.

Above all, Lord,
Let me look at faces
　　as you looked at them,
　　long ago,
　　when Scripture said of you:
　　he looked at him and he loved him.

Give me, Lord,
    a little of your infinite tenderness,
    only a little, I implore you.
Then, when I look at faces,
my gaze will be a warm caress.

Give me, Lord,
    a little of your purity.
Then, when I look at faces,
my gaze will be like sapphire on wax.
I'll release songs that have been hidden away for a long
    time
and I'll make long-buried agonies cry out,
    and tears will flow,
    smiles will radiate,
    and I,
    I'll listen to people singing or weeping
    and, ineffable mystery,
    I'll hear you, Lord,
    inviting me to sing or weep
    with them,
    with you, Lord.

Pathways of Prayer

Humans

Men and women have set up camp in a tiny little
corner of themselves. From time to time they venture
out of their tent to fetch some water from a stream
close by. But they never go beyond the boundaries of
their campgrounds.

Humans are undiscovered territory.

With Open Heart

How to help others

If you want to have a good influence on someone else, remember this golden rule: always be positive in your approach, never negative. Other people can be extremely sensitive to the judgement of their friends and acquaintances. A show of indifference or a lack of confidence (or worse still, of contempt) is enough to delay or even paralyse someone else's personal development.

If you want to have a good influence on someone else, begin with a show of unfeigned love, otherwise you will get nowhere. Place complete confidence in them, come what may. Show your admiration – there is always something about another person that should be admired in a tangible way. Your feelings alone will not suffice in this regard; you must express it. Silence can seem like a sign of disapproval to another person.

Never say to yourself: *I'm better than this person*, but rather, *They are better than I am in this particular regard*. Thus, instead of discouraging them from the outset, you will give encouragement.

Praise, when sincerely given, has an almost magical power to transform. If you want to see someone else make progress towards full maturity, congratulate them on their accomplishments, but do it sincerely. There are always opportunities for such praise. Take a good look at the other person. Make a just evaluation

of their good points and their abilities and bring them
into the open, for many are probably hidden, some
due to neglect, others due to a defeatist attitude.

In seeking out the good points in another person
and in praising them, you are not being a hypocrite,
but rather you are praising the Father. When you
want to see the religious dimensions of another
person – that is, when you approach them in the light
of your faith – you are on the road that leads to God,
for he is the giver of all good gifts.

Always place confidence in the other person,
despite temptations to the contrary or despite their
disappointing failures. If you tell them in so many
words that they are good for nothing, they will
become just that because you've convinced them that
it's true, and so they give up trying.

If in spite of everything you find it necessary
to reprove someone else or to condemn a certain
attitude or a certain action, begin by praising them for
something worthwhile they have done. Reproof on
its own embitters and even leads to discouragement.
It's not a question of condoning evil, but rather of
encouraging good. Don't keep poking about in the
ashes, but rather look for the flickering coals and fan
them into a blazing fire again. Be glad to see even the
slightest sign of progress.

If you want to have a good influence on someone
else, forget yourself. God has been busy at work and
it is he who saves and redeems. To influence another

person means going directly to the all-powerful Lord of love, who alone transforms the heart. Recall the words of St Paul: 'Where offence has abounded, grace has abounded yet more.' No one ever falls so low that the love of God is powerless to raise them up.

The Christian Response

Like a child

I played with a child who laughed a lot. I laughed along with them. Together, affectionately, we were at peace.

I wondered why we are so disarmed by the sight of a smiling child. I decided it's because our defences are down.

People with power scare us. We're afraid they might use their power against us, so we think about being more powerful than them, well-armed, just in case.

A child inspires love; disarmed as we are before it, our hands and hearts are free to reach out and love it.

If only we could all be like little children...

With Open Heart

The sea

Lives that are effective are not always the ones that attract attention. They are never those of the proud who storm against obstacles that cannot be removed. Lives lived humbly, under the eyes of God, illumined by his grace and radiant with love for others, are always effective.

Lord, I saw the sea attacking the rocks, sombre and raging.
From afar the waves gained momentum.
High and proud, they leapt, jostling one another to be the first to strike.
When the white foam drew back, leaving the rock clear, they gathered themselves to rush forward again.

The other day I saw the sea, calm and serene.
The waves came from afar, creeping, so as not to draw attention.
Quietly holding hands, they slipped noiselessly and stretched at full length on the sand to touch the shore with the tips of their beautiful soft fingers.
The sun gently caressed them, and they generously returned streams of light.

Lord, grant that I may avoid useless quarrels that tire and wound without getting anywhere.

Keep me from these angry outbursts that draw
attention but leave one uselessly weakened.

Keep me from wanting always to outstrip others in
my conceit, crushing those in my way.
Wipe from my face the look of dark, dominating
anger.
Rather, Lord, grant that I may live my days calmly
and fully, as the sea slowly covers the whole shore.
Make me humble like the sea, as, silently and gently,
it spreads out, unnoticed.
May I wait for my brothers and sisters and match my
pace to theirs, that I may move upwards with them.
Grant me the triumphant perseverance of the waters.
May each of my retreats turn into an advance.
Give my face the light of clear waters.
Give my soul the whiteness of foam.
Illumine my life that it may sing like sunbeams on the
surface of the sea.

But above all, Lord, may I not keep this light for
myself, and may all those who come near me return
home eager to bathe in your eternal grace.

Prayers of Life

If you are discouraged

You're discouraged because somewhere in your life, or in the lives of others, love has failed. If you want to recover, you must try offering a loving gesture. It will put you back on the road to hope, and life. For a failed love is like death, and love itself is life.

With Open Heart

Severed ties

Severed ties always create anguish. Think how a spider panics when one of the strands of its cobweb is broken. In the same way, people panic and suffer when their ties with nature, with other people, with God are broken. They lose their sense of security. They're cut off from their lifeline. Hurt and frightened, they lose their self-control. Like shipwrecked people, they frantically search for something to hold on to – but there's nothing strong enough to carry their weight, so they drown.

Ties between people must be remade.

With Open Heart

Open my eyes, Lord!

The world and the people in it challenge and disturb us. We would like to know everything there is to be known about what lies beyond our own horizons, but we only see the surface of things and of human beings. To go deeper and to see as God sees, we need a different way of looking. Only the 'eyes of faith' – in other words, the eyes of Jesus Christ grafted onto our human eyes – can bring us his light and enable us to undertake this long pilgrimage.

Then, little by little, we will see the spirit of Jesus working throughout the course of human history and in its smallest details, and we will see his great body, which is born, develops, dies and rises each day. No longer will we contemplate simply Jesus of Nazareth, but Christ unfolding in the course of history – his mystery of creation, incarnation and redemption – and we can be joined to him through every part of our lives and that of our brothers and sisters to work with him and to build up his father's kingdom.

Lord,
I wish you would give me immense eyes
    to look at the world!
Because I'm looking, Lord.
I like looking

but my eyes are small,
too small
to see what lies beyond things,
men and women and events.

I look and I wonder about life,
    but I see only the outer shell,
    which is hard and sometimes rough.
Love beckons,
    but I contemplate
    only some of the flowers and fruits
    while the vital spirit escapes me.
And I suffer behind the thick glass of my window,
    I bang into it
    and sometimes I hurt myself badly
when a mist rises in my heart
    and clouds my way.
Lord, why have you given us eyes
that can't see,
    can't see your life beyond life,
your love beyond love?

Sometimes I seem to catch a few glimmers
    and then, mysteriously,
    words somewhat more beautiful
    than ordinary words
    are born in my heart,
words that dance and whirl,
trying to escape from their gilded cage.

They fly from my lips
and I try to catch them,
to tell myself and to express
what I'm wondering about…
what I expect…
what I'm getting near…
without being able to grasp it.
But the words are little birds, too small;
I hold it against them that they don't know how to sing
the song of the infinite,
for me and for others.

Then sometimes
I close my eyes willingly, for a long while,
and in the quiet of the night
I catch a glimpse of
a little of that light
that is hidden from me by day.
Then I see without seeing,
I believe.
But Lord, you have given me
eyes to look at my brothers and sisters,
feet to walk towards them
and to tread the good earth with them!
Lord, can I walk with my eyes closed,
shutting out the day?
I want to see when I look,
but my eyes are small,
too small

to contemplate what lies beyond.
Lord, give me immense eyes
    to look at the world.

Open my eyes, Lord,
    that I may see...
farther than the light of the rising sun,
which suddenly tinges nature
with the soft gleam of a young girl's face;
farther than the light of the setting sun,
when streaks of night sketch
    the shadow of wrinkles on the earth,
like the years on a weather-beaten face...
    that at last I may see
    the reflection of your infinite light.

Open my eyes, Lord,
    that I may see...
beyond the radiance of the silently smiling rose,
beyond the hand that offers it to me,
and the heart beyond the hand,
and the care that goes beyond even the heart
    ...that I may see, at last,
the reflection of your love.

Open my eyes, Lord,
    that I may see...
beyond human bodies
    that attract or repel,

beyond their eyes and their glances
 that light up or become dim,
    troubled hearts,
    joyous hearts.
And farther than the hearts of flesh,
    the flowers of love,
and even the wild grasses
    that we so quickly name as sins
    ...that I may see, at last,
    the children of the good God,
    coming into the world and growing up
    beneath the loving gaze of Our Father.

    Open my eyes, Lord,
    that I may see...
farther than the roads used by heavy trucks,
    the night,
when a thousand lights escape from hot factories;
farther than the ribbons of smoke
    tossed by the wind,
    above chimneys
    pointed towards the unattainable sky,
beyond those disturbing beauties,
    cities of the future,
where men and women ceaselessly remake the face of
the earth
    ...that I may see, at last, and hear
    the heartbeat of thousands of workers
    who complete the creation with you.

Open my eyes, Lord,
    that I may see...
beyond the inextricable dove-tailing
of human roads without number,
    roads that go uphill or down,
    expressways or blind alleys,
    red traffic lights,
    green traffic lights,
    'no entry' signs and speed limit signs;
roads east, west, north and south,
    roads leading to Rome,
    to Jerusalem
    or to Mecca,
farther than the millions who have travelled them
for thousands of years,
and farther than the stupendous mystery of their
freedom
    which casts them,
    thinking,
    loving,
    on the paths of life
    leading to the crossroads of their destiny
    ...that I may see
    your Calvary raised on high,
overlooking the central crossroads of the world,
    and you,
    down from your cross,
risen from the dead and travelling all these roads of
Emmaus,

where so many men and women walk alongside you
without recognising you,
    except for the few, in your word
    and in the breaking of bread;
    that I may finally see
    your great body growing,
    in the breath of the spirit
    and with Mary's motherly help,
    until that day when you present yourself to the
    Father
    at the end of time,
    when you, my great Jesus,
    will have reached
    your full height.

But I know, Lord, that in this world
I must see without seeing,
and that as long as I am on this earth
I will be a pilgrim of the invisible with heart
unsatisfied.
    I know also that it is not until tomorrow
    when I pass through the portals of night
    and see you at last as you really are,
    in your light,
that I will see what you see.
I must wait a while longer and walk in the half-
light...
But if it is your will, Lord,
    that this my prayer,

confided to so many friends
who will share it,
should not be just so many empty words,
I beg you,
I beseech you,
give us immense eyes
to look at the world,
and we will see a little of what lies beyond,
and those who look at us
will see what you see.
Then perhaps we will be able to say to them at last:
It is he, Jesus Christ,
the Light of the World.

Pathways of Prayer

She said to him: 'I'll be with you, my child'

Jesus is present in our lives – we are told this repeatedly. Do we really believe it or do we only half believe it? But whether we are at the beginning of our relationship with him or deeply committed to our life of friendship with him, we always suffer because we can't see or touch him.

We need to understand that physical presence is not the only way in which people are present to each other. Those who love each other authentically have experience of this.

It is love that makes people present to each other, and the intensity of their presence depends on the intensity of their mutual love.

God, who loves all of us infinitely, is totally present to each one of us.

Long ago, there were morning and evening prayers that began with the words: 'Let us place ourselves in the presence of God and adore him.' Our lives would be transformed if we developed the habit of placing ourselves in the presence of God frequently during the course of the day.

The man was leaving, Lord, to go I don't know where,
to live I don't know what important moment of his life.
    Leaning towards his elderly mother,
    he kissed her tenderly,
    and she
    kissed him even more tenderly.
Then, holding his face between her trembling hands,
    she whispered:
    'Go, my child, I'll be with you.'
There was a long silence...
then she added:
    'Do you believe that?'
    'Yes, Mother,' he said.
    He left.
And she,
with tears in her eyes,
accompanied him from a distance.

Some time later the man told me
that it was like this
whenever he went away,
and that he was always strengthened
in times of difficulty
by the belief that he was accompanied
by his mother's love.

    And as I meditate
    this evening,
    I suddenly realise, Lord,

that these are the words
    you used
    when you were leaving us
    to return to the Father:
'I will be with you ... until the end of time.'
And I'm sure that you expect us to respond
as the son responded to his mother:
    Yes, we believe it.

You know that I'm weak, Lord,
    and often,
    in difficult moments,
I look for the support of a friendly presence.
    I feel the need of a word,
    of a hand to hold,
    of a face to kiss,
but now I understand
that physical presence
is not necessarily the sign of real presence.
    Two people can see each other,
    touch each other
    and even embrace each other warmly
    while at the same time remaining at a distance,
    far from each other,
    separated from each other,
    unless their love,
    deep down,
    unites them.
How many handshakes are just play acting!

How many couples,
who have slept in the same bed for ages,
are just two lonely people
camping on one side or the other
of an impassable moat!

But I also believe, Lord,
with all my strength,
that two people
separated by time or space
can be together,
can be united,
can live in deep communion
if their love is alive.

I believe this of human beings, Lord,
so why shouldn't I believe it of you?
Since you love us infinitely,
your presence to each one of us
must be infinite.
Real presence,
total presence,
always and everywhere.

Nothing can separate us from you, Lord,
nothing that comes from you,
but only what comes from us

and above all…
our lack of faith.
This evening, Lord,
you are saying to me once again:
'I will be with you until the end of time'
and you are asking me quietly,
'Do you believe that?'
Yes, Lord, I do believe it,
but please increase my faith.

Let me always live
in your loving presence,
you who accompany me in my daily comings and
goings,
as the elderly mother
accompanies her son with her faithful love.
Help me to work in your presence,
to rejoice in your presence,
to rest in your presence,
because if I thought you were there, Lord,
if I was open to the love you offer,
I would never be alone again,
I would never be weak again,
and in front of you I would never be able
to do the bad things I'm tempted to do,
not like the little boy
who is afraid that his mother
will see what he is doing and punish him for it,

but like the grown-up son
who discovers his mother's great love for him
and then only wants to thank her for it
    through his life.

Pathways of Prayer

The power of love

I was called recently to the bedside of a dying man. He was very old and his face was ravaged and distorted by illness and suffering. I watched his wife. She was leaning over him, caressing him and whispering to him such tender words: 'How beautiful you are, my love, how fine you look!' I was embarrassed and thought: 'How can anyone be so blind? Love is blind!'

Then an extraordinary thing happened. As she caressed him, the old man half-opened his eyes and a hesitant smile appeared on his face. He looked at his wife for a long time and she looked at him. There was a mysterious communion between them. And his smile spread. It was like the sun after a storm. I saw it. I know that I saw what she saw! She was right – the old man, made ugly by suffering, was beautiful. Love is not blind – love lets us see what others do not see.

That woman was guided by love to go beyond the deep wrinkles of her husband's suffering face and had joined someone who was beyond, far beyond, the body, someone who could not die even if his body were to crumble away in her sight and finally disappear.

With Open Heart

We haven't finished loving each other

For husbands and wives who have loved each other and lived their lives together, nothing is harder than the separation of death. However, they haven't finished loving each other, because the loved one who is gone is still living in another life beyond death, and love cannot die when it is an authentic love in Christ.

But loving without the physical presence of the loved one is a terrible trial, a 'purgatory' – the last purification of love before people meet again in eternity. Happy are those who, though left alone, continue to be faithful and continue to live out their love (which does not mean, of course, that to rebuild one's life is to be unfaithful). To their children and to all those who have doubts about love or don't even know what love is, such people may testify that love can live and flourish beyond the two bodies of those who go through life together. They can also testify that at the final stage of its development, such love is given freely: 'I miss them, but I'm happy that they are happy!'

May such love help those who lack love.

I woke up, Lord
　　…and he wasn't there any longer.
I turned over in bed
　　…but his place was empty
and my lonely fingers were still searching for his.

My love is with you;
　　I believe he is – this is what I hope for –
but Lord, I can't
　　get used to his absence.
I'm torn apart every time I wake up,
　　just as waking up
shatters the patient whose legs have been amputated.

　　He's not there any longer!

I won't hear him any more.
I'll no longer share
　　the day's work with him.
I'll never again go over the furrows and wrinkles
　　on his beloved face,
　　furrows and wrinkles where I used to glean life,
　　the last grains of life,
　　which day after day
　　in joy and sorrow
　　we planted
　　and harvested
　　a thousand fruits of love.
I'll never again search in the depths of his eyes

for the soft lift of his twilight gaze,
    after the bright morning,
    the blazing midday fires,
    and the occasional shadows
    of days when clouds built up
    and the storm erupted,
before the rainbow of peace
rose in our hearts.

We loved each other ... but Lord,
we haven't finished loving each other!

We loved each other, Lord,
but we lived together;
he was in me and I was in him,
and you,
    you sealed our two lives together
    so that they became one.
But he has gone to those distant shores
    that no one can reach
    without passing through death,
and from the shore where I'm standing with my feet on
this earth,
I can't even catch a glimpse of him.
    Oh my beloved ... gone,
    far away,
    in the mists of infinity.

    He's not there any longer!

They say that one gets used to it, Lord,
that time does its work,
    but I know now
that neither time nor death can vanquish love,
    because one morning I whispered *always*,
    and he said to me *always*,
    and you promised us
that we would love each other forever.
Without seeing, Lord,
I want to believe,
    I do believe.

    We haven't finished loving each other!

Yesterday we were together,
    every day,
    learning about living,
because while each of us was seeking the other's
happiness,
    often we were seeking our own;
sometimes we gave and sometimes we took from the
other,
    but through our constant efforts
    our love was increased.

Today we have entered into purgatory.
    I suffer because I'm alone,
    he suffers because he's far away;

how could he be happy without me
when I'm so unhappy without him?

But he is purifying our love
in your light, Lord,
 whereas for me
 it is during the night
 that I must perfect it.

Help me, my God,
To love him even more today
 in his absence
 than yesterday in his presence;
to love him for himself, expecting nothing in return,
 happy that he's happy,
 close beside you;
 and gaining nothing for myself
 except joy in his joy.

Yes, my love is intact in my living heart.
 Death can do nothing to it,
 and that is why I'm suffering;
 because my spring has not run dry.
 It flows and overflows
and I have loving words to spare
 and a thousand gestures of affection,
smiles stored up that remain unemployed
and tears falling like rain, which flood my heart

and make all these flowers of love
spring up more quickly still.

Lord, I won't allow them
    to wither,
    to fade
    in my closed heart.
I'll gather them every day,
a wonderful harvest for my children
    and my grandchildren,
    my friends,
    my neighbours
    and all the forgotten beggars
    who search for fragments of love
    on the wayside.

But my suffering, Lord,
is still my suffering!
The dreadful loneliness and the long days
and the deep night,
    the absence,
the cruel absence,
the deep void into which my distraught heart plunges
without reaching the bottom.
    I miss him, Lord, do you understand?
    I miss him.
    Why have you abandoned me?

Forgive me, Lord.
Forgive me for being despondent,
you who beckon me from your cross every day.
It's when I forget to look at you
    that the night overwhelms me.
    You are waiting for me
    and he is there beside you, watching me,
    and with his love he invites me,
    guides me and supports me.

Thanks to you, Lord,
thanks to him,
my suffering won't be lost,
because I'll offer the superabundance of love
    that my suffering demands of me,
    love which lives and grows beyond my suffering;
I'll offer it for those young explorers of love
    who seek without finding,
    losing their way, innocents
    caught in the mirage of the moment;
for those who don't know, Lord,
that loving means
    leaving selfishness aside so as to give one's self to the
    other
    and being ready to receive the other's gift of himself;
for those who don't know
that love is often suffering
    before it is joy,
joy in the new life which takes flesh

when two lives join together,
   without ever destroying the love they share;
for those who don't know
that love is forever,
   and that only you can give
   this love its infinite dimension.

I'd like to say this to them, Lord,
   to say it to them through my life,
and since my beloved is waiting for me beside you,
   in peace, I also
   will await our meeting,
   and of this engagement,
   of this cruel and sweet encouragement,
of this waiting I'll make an offering
before I'm taken in the arms of my faithful love,
   before we love each other at last,
   Lord,
   in your house,
   infinitely, eternally.

Pathways of Prayer

Eyes

Eyes have great power, for they are conveyors of the soul. When God dwells in a person, their eyes can carry God to other people.

I am now about to close my eyelids, Lord,
for my eyes this evening have finished their work
and will return home,
having walked for a day in the garden of men and
women.
Thank you, Lord, for my eyes, windows open on the
wide world;
thank you for their look that carries my soul, as the
broad sunbeam carries the light and warmth of your
sun.
I pray to you during the night that tomorrow,
when I open my eyes to the clear morning,
they shall be ready to serve both my soul and my God.

May my eyes be clear and straightforward, Lord,
and give others a hunger for purity;
may my look never be one of disappointment,
disillusionment,
despair;

but may it know how to admire,
contemplate,
adore.
May my eyes learn to close in order to find you more
easily;
but may they never turn away from the world because
they are afraid.
May my eyes be penetrating enough to recognise your
presence in the world,
and may they never shut on the afflictions of men.

May my eyes be firm and steady,
but may they also know how to soften in pity and be
capable of tears.

May my gaze not soil the one it touches,
may it not disturb, but may it bring peace.
May it not sadden, but rather may it transmit joy.
May it not attract in order to hold captive,
but rather may it persuade others to rise above
themselves to you.

May my eyes disquiet the sinner because in them they
will see your light,
but may their reproach lead to encouragement.
Grant that my eyes may be startling because they are
an encounter,
an encounter with God.

Grant that they be a call,
a clarion call,
that brings all the world to its doorstep,
not because of me, Lord,
but because you are to pass by.

That my eyes may be all this, Lord,
once more, this evening,
I give you my soul,
I give you my body,
I give you my eyes,
that in looking at other people
it may be you who looks at them
and you who beckons.

Prayers of Life